Housesteads Rc

James Crow

CONTENTS

Tour of Housesteads

OVERVIEW OF THE FORT

Housesteads was originally surrounded by a high curtain wall 1.4m wide, backed by a rampart of earth which stood at least 4.25m up to the rampart walk. Major towers at the fort's four rounded angles enabled observation along the curtain wall, and, on the north side, along the line of Hadrian's Wall. Access was restricted to the four main gates. Arranged on a regular grid plan, the interior of the fort had all the formality and order of a military town on the edge of the empire. The main internal road led from the east gate – the principal entrance – towards the headquarters and intersected with a north–south road between two opposing gateways. Well-drained cobbled streets ran between the barracks and other buildings, including workshops and storerooms, and around the interior of the fort's defences, providing space for wheeled traffic and general circulation, and with room to muster in times of danger. To the west were six buildings, including five barracks. Across the central range were the buildings housing the garrison's administration and support functions, including the headquarters, commanding officer's house, granaries and hospital. To the east were five barracks and from about AD 300, the large 'building 15'. Altogether the barracks accommodated up to 800 men.

Above: Keystone with Atlas carrying the globe flanked by Victories, symbolizing Roman imperial domination with divine aid
Below: Reconstruction drawing of the fort and the surrounding civilian settlement in the early third century, seen from the south

Facing page: View along the surviving line of Hadrian's Wall in the Knag Burn and up to the north-east angle of the fort, which was overlooked by a high tower in Roman times

Top right: Watercolour of the west gate in 1850, by HB Richardson. The two outer passageways are among the best preserved gateways along the line of Hadrian's Wall
Above: The L-shaped slots for the beam which secured the gate on the inside can be seen on the central pier
Below: Plan of the west gate. At the outside corner of the south passage, setting-out lines on one of the stone footings show that there was a change of plan between the foundations being laid and the gate being completed

▮ WEST GATE

The west gate stands part way up the hill, beyond the remains of the commanding officer's house and the hospital, along the west curtain wall. The Roman road known as the Military Way ran out directly to the west, although in the late Roman period, after the gateway was blocked, banks and ditches were cut across the line of the road to provide greater protection for the defences. Like all the main gates at the forts along Hadrian's Wall the west gate was a double-arched gateway set between flanking gate towers. The gateway was set almost in line with the curtain wall and the superstructure of the gate would have risen high above the adjacent curtain wall and dominated the approach from the west. It enabled goods carts to access the granary, which they could not do from the other fort gates.

The passage walls of the gates were built of small squared stones similar to those from the curtain wall and Hadrian's Wall itself. These stones were set in mortar and laid in regular stone courses (but have been relaid or pointed using modern materials). These blocks could have been handled easily by a single builder. By contrast the stone blocks of the gateway itself are far larger and grander, conveying the sort of robust strength seen in Victorian viaducts. Legionaries, rather than auxiliaries (see page 12), would have undertaken the skilled building work. The threshold blocks are especially well preserved, particularly in contrast to those of the south and

West Gate

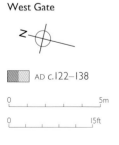

N

▨ AD c.122–138

0 ——————— 5m
0 ——————— 15ft

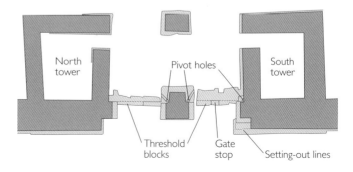

North tower

Pivot holes

South tower

Threshold blocks

Gate stop

Setting-out lines

east gates, where there is plenty of evidence for later repairs and rebuilding indicative of continual use. This suggests that the west gate was used less regularly and that the entire gateway was blocked in the late Roman period, making it harder for stone to be robbed-out for reuse in medieval or later times. When the gate was cleared in the 19th century, excavators found piles of stone roof tiles which had collapsed before the gateway was walled up.

2 ANGLE TOWER, BAKERY AND 3 TRACES OF BARRACKS

Below the turf in the western third of the fort, 19th-century excavators traced the remains of barracks. When the grass is newly mown, or especially dry, the platforms for the barracks are visible. The walls of the west curtain wall are especially well preserved. To the south is the outline of the angle tower, with the remains of a bakery later built into the fort rampart. Two horseshoe-shaped ovens are visible, each oven probably served the soldiers living in the two barracks nearby, running west to east (buildings 5–6) across the perimeter road. Up to 80 men lived in each barrack under the command of a centurion.

Each soldier was given a ration or *modius* ('measure') of wheat. The soldiers would have had to grind the wheat before making loaves and baking them in communal ovens (one for each century). In a letter found at Vindolanda, a fort just south of the Wall, there is a reference to wheat being issued for making 'turtas', or twisted loaves. Ordinary soldiers would have had a good diet, including meat, vegetables and cheese, and evidence from Vindolanda shows they were fond of beer. Imported foods were available for officers and from traders.

Above: The Carvoran modius, *a bronze measure found at the Wall fort at Carvoran which may have been used to check that the soldiers received the correct ration of grain*

Left: Reconstruction drawing of a bakery with a domed oven, set into the earth rampart of the defences
Above: The remains of a horseshoe-shaped oven in a bakehouse against the west wall of the fort

4 NORTH CURTAIN, 5 TURRET 36B AND 6 NORTH GATE

Above right: View west along the north curtain wall

A *Turret 36B*

B *Foundations of Building 7, overlying part of the turret walls*

C *Remains of later rampart building*

D *Expansion of the curtain wall*

Further along the west curtain wall lies the north-west angle tower, and from the crest of the ridge the line of Hadrian's Wall is visible, running off west along the crags and into the pine wood. Milecastle 37 lies 400m to the west, reached either by a path alongside the Wall, or by following the Roman Military Way. To the north, open rough pasture extends as far as the horizon, marked by the Kielder and Border forests.

Building Hadrian's Wall

The construction of Hadrian's Wall began in AD 122 and teams of builders from the legions began work in the east around Newcastle and in the west from Carlisle. Initially the barrier from Carlisle to the river Irthing, where good stone was less readily available, was made from cut turf blocks.

Regularly spaced one Roman mile (1,472m) apart was a series of small forts, known as milecastles. These are now numbered from 1 to 80 onwards along the Wall's 80 Roman miles from the east – the milecastle at Housesteads is number 37.

Between each milecastle were two watch towers, or turrets, identified by their nearest wall-mile, and the one built before work began on the fort is Turret 36B. As construction of the Wall progressed, the original plans were modified. In the central sector across the Whin Sill Crags only a broad foundation was laid, and parts of the turrets and milecastles were built at the same time. Only later in Hadrian's reign was the Wall completed at a narrower width of 2.5m. This building sequence is quite clear at Housesteads.

Above: Some Roman building tools – a plumb bob weight, a hammer and a chisel

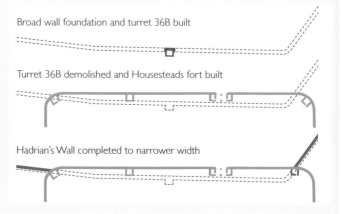

Broad wall foundation and turret 36B built

Turret 36B demolished and Housesteads fort built

Hadrian's Wall completed to narrower width

The line of Hadrian's Wall was laid down before the building of the fort and continues east along the crest as far as the traces of Turret 36B, displayed, along with the foundations of the Wall, in a hollow in the turf. The fort wall was set forward of the crest, probably to ensure that the granaries were on a level, well-drained site. Along the inner face of the north curtain wall are two scars, marking the side walls of an interval tower, and set back from the curtain wall is the outline of a stone-lined water tank. At Housesteads, these are found at several points at the base of the rampart beside the perimeter road inside the fort and were designed to catch rainwater, as there were no perennial springs at sufficient height to provide an aqueduct for the garrison. Within this water tank, however, are a number of slabs, set on edge, defining a long rectangle against the tank's north side. These are the remains of a cist burial (see page 40). Nearby, a small stone building with a curved end, now covered over, was excavated at the end of the 19th century. This was probably a small Christian chapel which dates, together with the grave, to the final period of Roman occupation, probably in the early fifth century.

The main access to the fort from north of the Wall was by the north gate, just past Turret 36B. The layout of the gate is similar to that of the east gate and the inner central pier is well preserved. Of particular interest are the massive foundations seen on the outside, required to support the gatehouse. Originally a ramp led up from the gate but this was cleared away in the 19th century. A roadway led north-eastwards towards the valley of the Knag Burn but was abandoned in the later second century, probably because the climb was too steep, and a new gateway was built through Hadrian's Wall. Remains of a later postern gate can be seen in the west side of the gateway.

Above: Detail of a watercolour by HB Richardson (1848) showing the west side of the exterior of the north gate, a postern gate and John Clayton's foreman, William Rutherford

Below: The north gate and the line of Hadrian's Wall reaching eastwards across the Knag Burn towards Sewingshields. Local workmen in the mid 19th century reportedly said that the water tank shown in the foreground would have been used by the Romans 'to wash their Scotch prisoners in'

⑦ GRANARIES (*HORREA*)

Set back from the north wall and gate, the granaries are the most substantial remaining structures inside the fort. All Roman forts had such buildings to store sufficient supplies for the garrison and for soldiers out on campaign. The main commodity was grain, probably kept in sacks. Some cereal crops were grown in Northumberland and there are clear signs of Roman-period terraces and other fields in the vicinity of the fort. But other foods and wines were imported over wide distances to satisfy the appetites of the garrison.

At this period, goods access to the fort was by the west gate, with an open area in front of the granaries to allow carts to unload and turn. The granaries were built on high-level ground to ensure secure and well-drained foundations.

Above: Reconstruction drawing showing the granaries as they were first constructed under Hadrian

Below: The north granary. Buttresses against the outer walls probably supported a wide roof and the floor was raised on rough stone pillars to keep the foodstuffs dry

Hunting

From letters found at Vindolanda, we know that the officers, at least, enjoyed a varied diet, including venison. They were passionate about hunting and kept prized breeds of hounds. 'If you love me brother', wrote Vindolanda's commandant, Flavius Cerialis, to his friend Brocchus, 'I ask you to bring me hunting nets ... be sure to mend them very strongly'. From the high Pennine moors south of Housesteads, an altar to Silvanus, the god of huntsmen, was dedicated by an exultant cavalry commander to commemorate his success at bagging an 'exceptionally fine boar which many of his predecessors had been unable to hunt down'.

The remains of two separate long buildings, with entrances facing the west, survive but the original Hadrianic structure was a wide single hall, divided by a single row of six stone piers. Its bases and capitals can be seen between the two later walls. The outside walls were strengthened by regular buttresses supporting the wide-projecting eaves of the roof.

The double-aisled granary was rebuilt with parallel cross-walls, representing two separate buildings, and a stone with the initials of the First Cohort of Tungrians (see page 12) was reused in the new south wall indicating the Tungrians' earlier presence at the fort. Six fragments of a monumental inscription from the time of Septimius Severus (AD 193–211) are known from other locations at the fort and may relate to this major rebuilding.

The regular rows of upright stones seen inside the north granary were used to raise the timber floor to keep the food dry and to some extent safe from vermin, while vents in the outside walls ensured air circulated. By the fourth century the north granary seems to have gone out of use, since there is little wear on the threshold, and the south granary had been converted into accommodation, with only a small part still operating as a granary at the east end.

*Above: Second-century jasper intaglio, or engraved gemstone, from a finger ring found at Housesteads, depicting a huntsman with hare suspended from his hunting stick (*lagobolon*)*

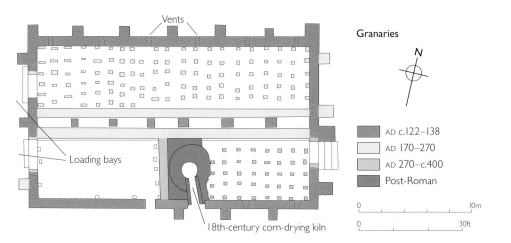

Vents

Loading bays

18th-century corn-drying kiln

Granaries

N

▨ AD c.122–138
▢ AD 170–270
▨ AD 270–c.400
▨ Post-Roman

0   10m

0   30ft

Above and right: Base of a stone column supporting the veranda along the length of the original barracks. Many are found reused in later buildings. The reconstruction drawing of barrack 13 (above right) shows the veranda and individual rooms opening onto the perimeter road and the north rampart

Below and facing page: Plans of the original and modified barracks. Some of the walls of the earlier barracks were reused, but in many instances the new walls were built over the demolished original structure

8 BARRACKS

A characteristic feature of Roman forts was the regular layout of the interior and the provision of barrack buildings for the ordinary soldiers. At Housesteads 10, or perhaps 11, such buildings are known. The cohort was divided into ten centuries and each barrack was allocated to a century of men (probably 80 in number), commanded by a centurion. The barracks were long and narrow, aligned east to west and normally subdivided into 10 rooms, or *contubernia*. Each *contubernium*, a term derived from the practice of soldiers sharing a tent on campaign, was divided by a central wall into an outer and inner room, with lodgings for eight men (although much of the time many may have been stationed elsewhere). A larger suite of rooms at the end of the barrack closest to the fort wall was intended for the centurion, who lived with his family and slaves, and had his own private latrine.

Traces of the outline plans of the barracks are known from the excavations in 1898, but in the north-east corner of the fort barracks 13 and 14, which were excavated between 1974 and 1981, give a more complete picture. Here their layout and the areas behind the fort wall demonstrate the major changes in organization and accommodation through the fort's history.

Original barracks

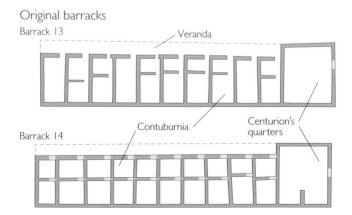

Barrack 13

Veranda

Contuburnia

Centurion's quarters

Barrack 14

Down the slope from the east side of the north gate is the line of barrack 13 and the traces of buildings behind the fort's north rampart. Across the street (laid out in gravel) is barrack 14, with traces of the later building 15 beyond that and the east gate. Along the north side of barrack 13 there were doorways for the individual rooms (*contubernia*) looking out under a veranda to the north rampart. The outlines of parts of this building can be traced, however, like the other barracks in the fort, towards the end of the third century, when parts of it were demolished and a new range of accommodation was constructed on the footprint of the earlier building.

The walls of the later structures, built of small, roughly squared stones bonded with earth and clay, were probably less than 1m high. The upper parts would have been built of timber with wattle and daub walls covered in rough plaster. Although the alignment of the later buildings follows that of the earlier barracks, a series of independent structures was built in its place. Their doorways still faced north, but they had side walls, separating them from the next building. These new barrack blocks reflect changes to the garrison which had probably been reduced to half of its former strength. The soldiers may have lived in these 'chalets' with their dependents.

Above: *Reconstruction drawing showing the line of individual 'chalets' constructed after AD 270 on the site of the earlier demolished barrack 14*

Modified barracks (original barracks shown in grey tone)

Barrack 13

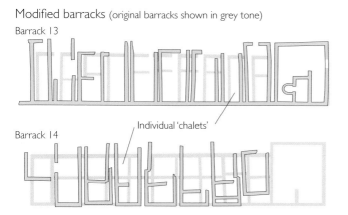

Individual 'chalets'

Barrack 14

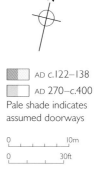

N

AD c.122–138

AD 270–c.400

Pale shade indicates assumed doorways

0   10m

0   30ft

The Garrison

The Roman army was one of the most successful fighting machines of the pre-industrial world. During the early empire soldiers were paid regular wages, served for fixed terms and received the benefits of secure, well-built accommodation.

The army was divided into legions and auxiliaries. The legions were recruited from Roman citizens and formed the core of the imperial campaign armies; each legion was about 5,500 men strong, including a number of specialists, among whom were those responsible for building Hadrian's Wall. In Britain their bases were at York, Chester and Caerleon, in south Wales.

Hadrian's Wall was garrisoned by auxiliaries – regiments of infantry and cavalry raised from the conquered peoples of the empire. It is likely that the infantry regiment, the *cohors I Tungrorum milliaria* ('the first cohort of Tungrians a thousand strong') was stationed here from the outset.

The Tungrians were a German people from the region of Tongres, in eastern Belgium. They fought at Mons Graupius in AD 83 during Agricola's campaigns in Scotland, when their skill at close fighting with swords is said to have helped decide the battle. Part of the unit was stationed on the Antonine Wall in the mid second century, but they returned to full strength at Housesteads by AD 160. From the third century the garrison was supplemented by German war bands from Frisia, east of the Rhine, now Holland and north Germany.

Above: Relief of an archer showing his composite bow and a quiver slung across his back

Right: Leather shoes were found near the temples at Chapel Hill, and fragments of leather tents from within the fort. This one-piece leather shoe was soled with lightweight iron hobnails (above)

ⓘ RAMPART AND ⓘ EAST GATE

The excavations of the north-east quarter also provided clear evidence for long-term changes in the defences and occupation of the fort. Initially the fort wall was backed by a rampart of soil, with a low retaining wall along the perimeter road. Later in the third century the rampart was removed to make space for a series of workshops built against the fort wall. By the end of the century there was greater concern for security and new towers or platforms were constructed between the north and east gates and the existing angle tower.

The east gate at Housesteads was the main gate of the fort, though similar in plan to the other gates, and led onto the main street aligned with the imperial shrine in the headquarters building. The first excavations of the east gate showed that the south portal was blocked in Roman times. To the north there are deep wheel ruts and a gate stop, rebuilt a number of times. The exterior façade was intended to impress, and there were reliefs of Victory and Mars with an impressive inscription recording its construction. The reconstruction drawing below shows a tiled roof on the flanking towers and across the gallery above the gateway, but it is equally possible there were open crenellated parapets on the towers and curtain wall.

The Military Way which linked the garrisons stationed along the Wall was normally set back from the Wall itself, but along the high ridge of the Whin Sill the road snaked up and down seeking an easy gradient for carts hauling their loads. From the east gate the road dips towards the Knag Burn gate and then climbs up in a broad sweep (see map on page 28).

Below: Relief sculpture of Victory, which once adorned the exterior of the east gate
Bottom: Reconstruction drawing of the interior façade of the east gate

11 BUILDING 15 AND 12 THE BATHS

South of barrack 14 the high standing masonry marks the east end of building 15. This large building displays some of the grandest stonework of any in the fort. Many of the blocks have distinctive cross-hatch dressing. Small notches in the upper faces show where the stones were levered into position. Building 15 probably occupied the site of a stable, the drains of which are buried deep below the flagged floor. The new building, which can be dated to the later third century, was a grand aisled hall with a central row of posts. There were doorways in the south and east sides, broad enough to allow a cart to enter and unload. The internal area is nearly twice that of the two earlier granaries, and building 15 may be compared with a great medieval tithe barn. Such buildings are uncommon in Roman Britain, but it was most likely an imperial storehouse, intended for the collection and distribution of taxes in kind: the imperial response to the rampant inflation of the later third century.

At the east end of this long hall, a small bathhouse was constructed in the later fourth century, the only new example of this period from Hadrian's Wall. Bathing was an important social activity in the Roman world and all the forts on Hadrian's Wall had bath buildings set outside the walls. The earlier baths at Housesteads were located to the east on the opposite bank of the Knag Burn, where there was a regular water supply. (Traces of these baths are known from earlier excavations, but have never been fully explored.) They were some way from the fort, and it seems that these were abandoned, perhaps for greater security, as some stones from the earlier baths were used in the later one. The new baths were much smaller – either because the garrison was smaller or indicating a lessening of Romanized ways – and used water collected

The north-east quadrant of the fort

A *Barrack 13, showing the individual 'chalets' of the fourth-century barracks*

B *Barrack 14, shown in the same phase*

C *Building 15 and the small, late fourth-century bath suite at the east end*

D *The east gate*

E *The north-east angle tower*

F *Interval tower*

G *East side of the north gate*

from roofs and gutters. The baths building was an L-shaped structure with an entrance on the south side into a cold room, and a small cold bath in the corner. To the east was a warm room then a hot room, both with an underheated floor (hypocaust). The sequence of cold to warm to hot rooms was the same as that found in much larger bathhouses.

Some of the pillars survive and at the north end traces of the furnace can made out from the reddened stones, hacked out through the earlier wall. A rough phallus was carved for good luck on the side of the alcove. A stash of coal found during 19th-century excavations in the south side of the east gate was probably used to fuel the furnace.

Top: Reconstruction drawing of the small bathhouse at the end of building 15, showing the small cold bath, the warm room, the hot alcove, and the furnace room containing a copper boiler

Above: This glass flask found in the commanding officer's house would probably have contained bath oil

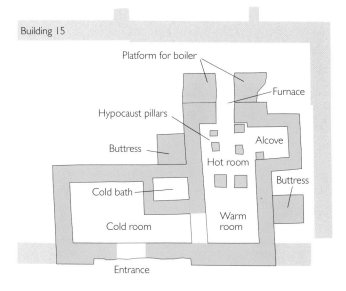

Building 15

Platform for boiler

Furnace

Hypocaust pillars

Buttress

Alcove

Hot room

Cold bath

Buttress

Cold room

Warm room

Entrance

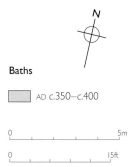

N

Baths

AD c.350–c.400

0   5m

0   15ft

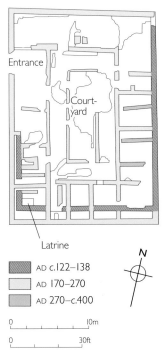

Right: Reconstruction drawing showing the enclosed courtyard in the hospital. Later the colonnade was demolished and the building was turned over to domestic use

Hospital

▣ HOSPITAL *(VALETUDINARIUM)*

A building constructed around a central courtyard, behind the headquarters, has been identified as a hospital. Stone from the north half of the building was removed to build a later farmhouse, shown on an 18th-century sketch by William Stukeley (see page 43). The main entrance lay to the west; rooms on all four sides opened onto a central courtyard, marked by the low rectangular wall that would have supported a colonnade. There is a large room to the north with smaller rooms around the east and south sides. The building appears to have been extended to the south, but the latrine in the south-west corner appears to have functioned in both periods.

   Although the building's function is not certain, the presence of a well-constructed latrine demonstrates that it was intended for accommodation, quite distinct from the barracks. Excavations at Wallsend revealed an almost identical building, probably similar in function. Auxiliary garrisons were provided with medical staff and a tombstone found at Housesteads records a surgeon called Anicius Ingenuus. The presence of such a building reflects the concern of the emperors for the welfare of their soldiers, since hospitals in Roman towns in Britain or elsewhere are unknown, outside of military camps. As elsewhere in the fort, in the fourth century there was a change of use. The north-east side of the central courtyard was paved over with flags, and there is evidence that the north room was used as a residence.

Entrance

Court-
yard

Latrine

N

AD c.122–138
AD 170–270
AD 270–c.400

0   10m
0   30ft

Roman Surgery and Medicine

A report of the First Cohort of Tungrians from the time they were stationed at Vindolanda in about AD 95 records that from a total strength of 752 men only 296 were present in the fort, of whom 15 were sick and 10 had an inflammation of the eyes. Eye infections were a commonly mentioned complaint – infections such as conjuncitivitis spread quickly in close quarters and from rarely changed water in the fort's warm baths. We know that the British fleet (*classis Britannica*) which helped to build part of Hadrian's Wall had its own eye doctor, Axius, whose eye ointment was mentioned by the great medical writer Galen. It contained copper and zinc hydroxide, zinc carbonate, opium and mercuric sulphide.

Anicius Ingenuus was attached to the First Cohort of Tungrians as a doctor with the rank of centurion '*medicus ordinarius*' and died at the age of 25 at Housesteads. It is not known whether Anicius had a more senior physician to report to or what other staff helped to run the hospital.

Although the Romans took some of their medical ideas from the ancient Greeks, and many men of Greek origin served as doctors in the army, their approach to military medicine was more pragmatic and focused on keeping the soldiers fit for combat with special expertise on dressing wounds and removing arrowheads. They also sought help from the gods: altars to the Greek healing god Asclepius are known from forts in north Britain and votive offerings in the shape of afflicted parts such as miniature hands and feet have been found at shrines in Britain. A whole range of medical instruments has been found on the Wall, including forceps, probes, hooks, surgical knives and evidence for a possible opthalmic needle.

Top: Medical instruments found at Housesteads, including on the left, a hollow spoon for administering medicine, and two ligulae on the right for mixing ointments or cosmetics
Above: Votive foot offered to the gods in the hope of a cure
Left: Tombstone of Anicius Ingenuus, medicus ordinarius of the First Cohort of Tungrians, who died at the age of 25

*Above: Relief of the god of war,
Mars, in an oval panel similar to the
shape of an auxiliary shield. Found in
the rubble of the headquarters
building, it was matched at the fort
entrance by a figure of Victory*
*Below: Reconstruction drawing of the
headquarters in the early third century*

▣ HEADQUARTERS (*PRINCIPIA*)

Roman civilization was essentially urban and, like the forum in a
Roman town, the headquarters of a fort was located centrally
at the junction between the two major roads: the *via praetoria*
from the main, east gate, and the *via decumana* linking the
north and south gates. The headquarters was a microcosm of
the administrative and religious functions found in an urban
forum and comprised three main elements: an entrance into a
courtyard lined on three sides with a colonnade; a cross-hall;
and beyond that five rooms across the rear of the building
including the central *aedes*, a shrine where the standards were
kept. At most forts the unit's strongroom was usually located
below this chamber, partly because the standard-bearer looked
after the soldiers' savings, but also because it was then provided
with divine protection. At Housesteads the bedrock was too
hard and so the strongroom was probably located in the north
room of the rear range, reached only from within the *principia*.

The headquarters occupies a narrow platform, buttressed
on the downhill south side by large monumental blocks, partly
restored after excavation in 1898. The east entrance and wall
have been extensively 'robbed', but a relief of Mars, now at
Chesters Museum, was found outside the building and had
probably fallen from the decorated entrance. Inside the

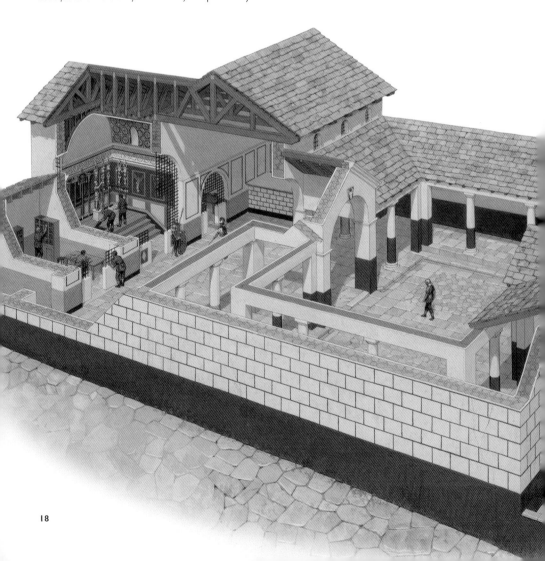

headquarters building the column bases mark the colonnade around the three sides of the courtyard. Later these spaces were closed up to make additional rooms with hearths. Although these changes now appear quite untidy it was probably covered with plasterwork. On the west side, the wall rose higher and had high clerestory windows to light the cross-hall. There would have been another elaborate entrance into the hall and the pivot stones for substantial wooden doors can be seen in the worn lintel. The cross-hall was a *basilica*, a covered assembly space with a raised platform or *tribunal* at the north end, and a moulded base for statues or inscriptions at the south. This was the place where orders and rosters, such as those surviving from Vindolanda, could have been posted, and justice administered by the senior officer.

The *aedes*, centrally placed against the rear wall of the building, was the official shrine for the worship of the emperor and the place where the unit's standards were kept. The standards were carried in battle, and were also venerated, being decorated with flowers and paraded on religious festivals. The shrine also contained statues of the emperor and the imperial family, as well as dedications to Jupiter, the god most associated with the imperial cult and the goddess Discipline. The headquarters building therefore combined both the symbolic and functional elements of the Roman forum. In the fourth century there were a number of changes; excavations showed that there was an upper storey over the rear range as flue tiles (for a heating system possibly from this period) found in the north room had fallen onto the lower floor, where bundles of arrowheads were stored.

Above: Some of the 800 iron arrowheads found in the debris from the north-west corner of the headquarters building

Headquarters

▨	AD c.122–138
☐	AD 170–270
▦	AD 270–c.400

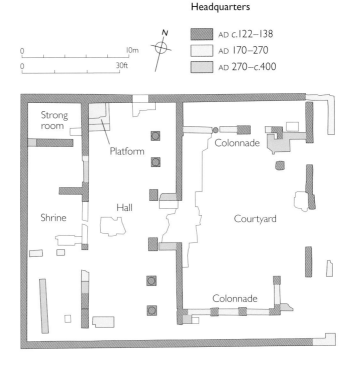

Strong room

Platform

Shrine

Hall

Colonnade

Courtyard

Colonnade

0 — 10m
0 — 30ft

N

Above: Small pottery beaker found in the drain of the commanding officer's house

Below: *Reconstruction drawing of the interior courtyard of the commanding officer's house, showing the prefect in conversation with the senior centurion*

15 COMMANDING OFFICER'S HOUSE (*PRAETORIUM*)

On the slope below the headquarters and next to the south gate are the remains of the commanding officer's residence (*praetorium*). This was the largest single building in the fort and the courtyard plan recalls the form of houses for the Roman elite in the western provinces of the empire. The commanding officer at Housesteads had the title of *praefectus* ('prefect') and the names of five such officers are known from dedications on altars. All were of equestrian rank and came from rich, landed, provincial families who could expect to serve in both civilian and military offices across the empire. Two were probably from southern Britain, one had a name known in central Italy and Croatia, and the origin of the final two cannot be ascertained. Large milliary cohorts of 800 men such as those at Housesteads were relatively rare and would have had a higher status than many of the regiments on the Wall, with the exception of cavalry. The size of the commanding officer's house reflects this, especially when compared with the barrack space allocated to soldiers and the modest rooms given to the centurions.

The builders faced the problem of creating a grand house on a challenging slope and, as elsewhere, many of the building's stones were later reused, making it a difficult structure for archaeologists to unravel. The house, which had a main east entrance from the *via principalis*, seems to have been laid out in two main phases. The first was an L-shaped building to the north and to the west when the courtyard house may have been completed in timber. Later the south and east sides were added using long stone blocks, laid in a distinctive pattern known as 'headers and stretchers'. A clear junction between the two phases is visible at the south-west angle.

Left: Aerial view of the commanding officer's house seen from the south-east, with parts of the headquarters and hospital also visible to the north

In the centre of the north range is a room with a flagged floor raised on stone pillars of a variety of shapes and origins. This was a dining room with underfloor heating and beyond was a kitchen. All these structures belong to the later phase of the house, and built into the oven was a fragment of the Severan inscription from the early third century thought to come from the granaries (see pages 9 and 38). On the west side were further rooms and a hypocaust, together with a latrine with a drain leading out under the west wall. Excavations have revealed small fragments of wall plaster, and, from the drain, fine pottery, glass fragments, coins and a gold signet ring, all indicating the high status of the residents. In the south-east corner a room with two drains is thought to have been a stable with a trough on the outside wall, close to the south gate and separated from the rest of the house.

The house underwent many alterations, reflecting the frequent changes of postings for the prefects who may have served for as little as three years (though short postings were the norm). Many of the alterations can be dated to the fourth century, thus providing important evidence for its continuing function as an elite residence into the later Roman period.

Roman signet ring
This gold signet ring with a garnet intaglio was found in the private latrine in the *praetorium* in 1968. Dating from the late first to second century, it is of high quality and would probably have belonged to the commanding officer. The stone, which was probably engraved abroad, features a theatrical mask as its subject.

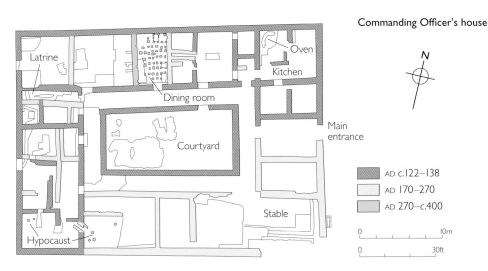

Commanding Officer's house

N

AD c.122–138
AD 170–270
AD 270–c.400

0 — 10m
0 — 30ft

16 LATRINES AND WATER SUPPLY

The communal latrines, in the south-east angle at the lowest point in the fort, are one of the most remarkable survivals of Roman fort planning in Britain. They were in a long and narrow building, whose side walls butted up against the interior of the fort wall, with the entrance on the west side. Inside, a deep sewer channel flows anticlockwise around a central platform to an outflow through the fort wall immediately west of the corner tower. Directly over the channel was a continuous row of lavatory seats – there was no privacy – and the sockets to support the stone or wooden seats can be seen on the south side. Elsewhere in the Roman world marble seating survives from public latrines. Once again here is a structure frequently found in Roman towns forming a key element of a frontier fort.

There was no external water source available to supply the hilltop garrison, and no aqueduct, such as that at Chesters and elsewhere, is known. As a result the latrines were situated in this low-lying area to take advantage of rainwater collected from roofs and streets and channelled into a series of drains to ensure the most efficient cleansing of the system. Such a system was effective only during and after rain and to provide

a more constant source a large water tank containing up to 23,800 litres was built across the doorway into the angle tower. It was carefully constructed with jointed sandstone slabs sealed with lead caulking, which survives in places. On the south-east side are two holes, at different levels, to allow water to drain into a channel leading into the latrines.

The grooved channel on the latrine's central platform runs in a clockwise direction to provide water for washing and empties at the south-east angle. It is often claimed that Roman soldiers used sponges instead of lavatory paper, but as it would have been necessary to import these from the Mediterranean, other materials such as moss were used instead. Replacement stone troughs were later brought in as water containers.

Among the debris excavated from the sewer pit was a broken sculpture of a dolphin and a pair of feet, probably from a figure of Neptune, now in Chesters Museum. Another sculpture of Neptune (now in Newcastle) shows the god reclining with three nymphs. A circular hole at the base shows that it was part of a fountain, although its location in the fort is not known. Both sculptures show how the Romans celebrated the benefits of water, as a source of life and for hygiene.

Above: A relief of a reclining Neptune, god of the sea, holding a small trident and a small dolphin, with three nymphs – part of a decorated fountain probably associated with the water tanks connected to the latrines

Facing page, top: Reconstruction drawing showing the communal latrines in use

Facing page, bottom: The latrines seen from the east. In the foreground are the water channels fed by a cistern beside the angle tower

Latrines and Water Supply

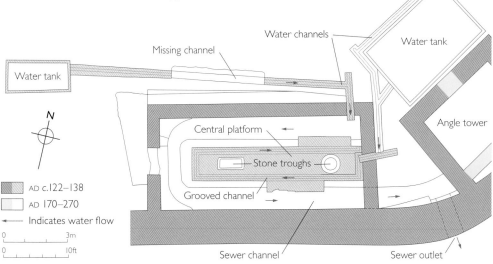

Water channels

Water tank

Missing channel

Water tank

N

Angle tower

Central platform

Stone troughs

AD c.122–138

AD 170–270

Indicates water flow

Grooved channel

0   3m

0   10ft

Sewer channel

Sewer outlet

Facing page, below and bottom:
Vicus buildings 1 and 2 located outside the south gate. The reconstruction drawing shows the division between the shop fronting onto the street, and the storeroom and living space behind

Below: *Part of a letter from Vindolanda written by a civilian trader supplying the army with a consignment of hides*

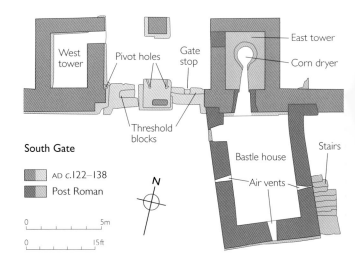

South Gate

AD c.122–138
Post Roman

0 ____ 5m
0 ____ 15ft

West tower · Pivot holes · Gate stop · East tower · Corn dryer · Threshold blocks · Bastle house · Stairs · Air vents · N

Octavius to his brother Candidus, greetings...The hides which you write are at Cataractonium [Catterick] – write that they be given to me and the wagon ... And write to me what is with that wagon. I would have already been to collect them except that I did not care to injure the animals while the roads are bad ... I hear that Frontinius Julius has for sale at a high price for leather-making the things which he bought here for five denarii a piece ...

⛌ SOUTH GATE

Although the east gate was formally the main entrance of the fort, the entrance most frequently used was to the south. The gate led directly out to the civilian settlement (*vicus*). On its east side the structure was much altered by a later defended farm or bastle house. South of the gate, buildings 1 and 2 of the *vicus* were built projecting across one side of the approach road, indicating that the east portal was already blocked and out of use by the early third century.

The east tower of the south gate was reoccupied in the later 16th century and extended to create a defended farmhouse, a type of building known in the Anglo–Scottish borderlands as a bastle. The ground floor was used as a defended byre for cattle. The living quarters for the farming family were located above and entered by steps from the north and on the east side. The door mouldings on the ground floor are quite distinct from Roman work. The interior of the Roman tower was used as a kiln for drying corn during the poor summers of the 'little Ice Age' in the 17th and 18th centuries.

⛌ CIVILIAN SETTLEMENT (*VICUS*)

Civilian settlements were found outside most forts in Britain. *Vicus* (plural *vici*) is a legal term in Latin denoting a settlement lower in status than a fully developed town. A fragmentary dedication from Housesteads with the letters D VICA... (see page 38) can be completed to mean 'by decree of the villagers', a rare insight into the organization of these settlements showing that the *vicus* at Housesteads had a formal status.

Although the fort today lies in an empty landscape, in Roman times a settlement of perhaps 500 people clustered around the southern flanks of the fort from the east gate around to the south-west corner. Further down the hillside to the south was a series of temples on the north side of the ridge known as Chapel Hill, situated midway between the fort

and the car park. In the 1930s more than 20 buildings were excavated, although only six remain on view.

Coins are much more commonly found in a fort such as Housesteads than in towns in Roman Britain because part of a soldier's pay was in cash. Although a portion would have been saved, there must always have been a small surplus available for entertainment and other purposes. Among those who followed the army were traders and merchants who procured oil, fish sauce and olives from the Mediterranean, as well as more local produce, such as the consignment of hides recorded in the Vindolanda letters. At Housesteads these merchants would have boosted the local economy and perhaps occupied the larger stone houses in front of the south gate. Elsewhere in the *vicus*

Gambling and Crime at Housesteads

Top right: Third-century mosaic from Thysdrus (El Djem, Tunisia) showing dice players
Above: *Bone dice (top), coin mould (middle) and counterfeit coin (bottom), all found in the* vicus *at Housesteads*

Rudyard Kipling imagined that the settlements next to the Wall forts formed 'a roaring and rioting town', and there is certainly evidence from Housesteads to support this view. House 2 next to the south gate may have been an inn, and crude dice have been found there. In house 4 a furnace at the rear was probably used to counterfeit coins, and moulds have been found elsewhere on the site.

A little further from the fort, in house 8, which may also have been a shop or inn, excavators in the 1930s made a gruesome discovery. Two skeletons had been dug into the clay floor of the rear room and covered with a clean layer of clay. One was a man with the tip of a knife in his ribs, and the other, more fragmentary, was probably a woman. All burials, apart from those of infants, were usually located beyond the settlement. There can be little doubt that this burial is evidence of a murder.

Violence was never far from soldiers, even outside the camps. The Roman poet Juvenal describes in Satire 16 how it is better not to admit that 'your smashed-in teeth, swollen face black and blue with bruises and the one eye left to you which the doctor is doubtful he can save' came from being beaten up by a soldier, else 'you will make enemies of the cohort' and risk being beaten up worse a second time round.

there may have been some retired soldiers and their families, as well as soldiers serving in the war band of Frisians who were based at Housesteads in the third century.

Immediately south of the south gate is a typical stone-built strip house (house 1), with the narrow side fronting onto the main road approaching the gate. Typical of many dwellings from towns in Roman Britain, the house is divided into two: a front room with a door and hearth, and a rear room with a basement below. In a later period an oven was built over the basement, which suggests the building may have been used as a bakery. Some of the latest coins found from the *vicus*, from no later than AD 320, were discovered in this house, indicating that it may have continued in use while most other buildings were abandoned. To the south is a building of similar size (house 2), possibly an inn, which has an entrance onto the street consisting of two stone sills with wel-preserved slots. These are typical of the fronts of Roman shops closed with shutters, examples of which survive from Pompeii.

Two other stone houses to the east front onto the roadway which passes by the south wall of the fort, as did other houses down the hillside. A domestic shrine was found in the corner of a yard behind house 12. Its carefully built stone apse contained a relief carving of three hooded gods, the *genii cucullati*, now in the Housesteads Museum. Further buildings are known to lie to the west, some of which were substantial stone structures, although many of these were found to be less well constructed, often of timber. To the west side of the south gate, a stone building with an unusual south-east angle was aligned to accommodate the existing road running south–west towards Vindolanda. The imposing blockwork masonry may suggest an official purpose.

Above: An iron 'lift' key found at Housesteads, the Roman equivalent of a front-door key. It would have had a wooden handle
Below: Relief of the genii cucullati (hooded deities) found in a shrine in the vicus and dating from the early third century. They wear the hooded cape, or byrrus Britannicus, a renowned export from Roman Britain

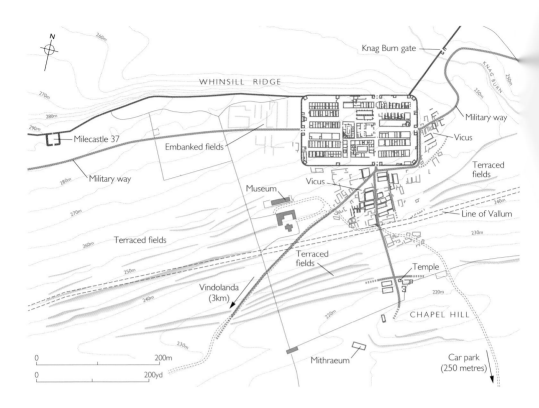

Above: *Plan of the fort in its wider landscape, including the network of Roman roads, the line of the Vallum and the extensive system of Roman terracing*

Below: *The Housesteads landscape photographed in 1907. Overlying the Roman fort, vicus and terraces are the remains of post-medieval farmsteads and fields. The present farmhouse was built by John Clayton in 1860*

Visible Roman remains

Excavated remains no longer visible

Remains known from aerial photography and survey

THE FORT IN ITS WIDER LANDSCAPE

Seen from afar, the rectangular outline of the fort appears to be draped across the high whinstone ridge, dropping abruptly to the north and falling more gently southwards, and into the valley of the Knag Burn, the garrison's main water source, to the east. Hadrian's Wall runs along the north side, from the east, climbing up from the Knag Burn and following the crest of the crags through the modern wood to the west and on towards Milecastle 37.

Outside the fort in Roman times the buildings of the civilian settlement were clustered in an arc around the perimeter walls. To the east and south the houses were aligned along a less regular pattern of streets and lanes, with ordered

embanked fields set out along the Military Way to the west. When the fort was first built the Vallum, a great ditched earthwork, ran across the southern fringe of the *vicus*, but it later fell out of use and was filled in by terraced fields, which may have provided food for the garrison. The climate was warmer than now and there is evidence of fields extending as terraces across the hillsides to the west and east. The sites of temples are known in the valley to the south, including a Mithraeum, dedicated to Mithras (see page 39), and another shrine to the German deities of the Frisian soldiers stationed here during the third century. The garrison's cemeteries cannot be located with any certainly but lay beyond Chapel Hill and along the main Roman roads leading away from the settlement.

KNAG BURN

The Military Way leads down from the east gate towards the valley of the Knag Burn. The burn flows through a Roman culvert set in Hadrian's Wall and next to it is a gateway, flanked by two internal towers. Gateways through the Wall are limited to the milecastles and forts, with other main gates located only where the two main provincial Roman roads crossed the Wall, north of Corbridge and near Carlisle.

At Housesteads the Knag Burn gate replaced the main north gate of the fort when access became too difficult, owing to the steep climb, in the later second century. Unlike the fort gates, here there were pairs of doors at the front and rear, to control access, and to provide additional security at a distance from the fort. Elsewhere in the Roman empire customs posts for trade and diplomatic exchange were restricted to one or two major frontier control points. At Housesteads and elsewhere along the Wall access through it was restricted to military purposes. Although some farmsteads are known to the north of the Wall around Housesteads, they are of uncertain date. While we might like to imagine that the Romans allowed access between the British communities divided by the Wall, there is little reason to assume that they would have done so.

Above: The Knag Burn gateway seen from the east. The gateway was built late in the second century and towers were added some time after that

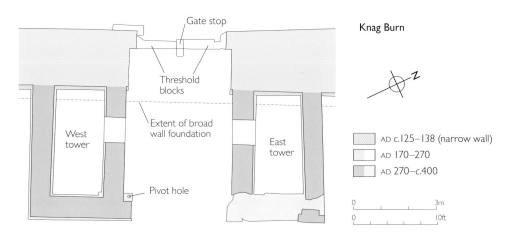

Gate stop

Threshold blocks

West tower

Extent of broad wall foundation

East tower

Pivot hole

Knag Burn

N

⬚ AD c.125–138 (narrow wall)
☐ AD 170–270
▨ AD 270–c.400

0   3m
0   10ft

Right: The north gate of Milecastle 37. Three of the arch stones, which can be seen in the reconstruction drawing on the facing page (top) have been restored

MILECASTLE 37

From the outside of the west gate the fort wall continues up to the line of Hadrian's Wall which leads west through the wood. This length of Wall was cleared in the 1930s and fallen stones were replaced to provide a level top. This method of conservation was employed from the 19th century onwards and survives in many places west from Housesteads, where Hadrian's Wall has a turf top. Beyond the wood the footpath runs alongside the Wall; the milecastle is tucked in a narrow cleft in the Whin Sill where there is a steep, but accessible, slope to the north.

The milecastle, first excavated in 1853, is a rectangular enclosure, on the south side of the Wall. There are two north and south gates, constructed with large masonry blocks similar to the fort gateways. The best preserved part is the north wall and gate with the remains of a barrack on the east side which could have held a garrison of up to 16 men. In the centre was an open space with timber buildings and hearths to the west.

A unique feature is the way in which the curtain walls taper from the broad gate piers to the narrow Hadrian's Wall, showing how the north gate and part of the broad foundation were left incomplete when construction first started on the fort. After the fort walls were finished, Hadrian's Wall was built at a narrow gauge up to the milecastle, which was also then completed. The south face of the north curtain wall still preserves the highest standing example of original Hadrian's

Milecastle 37

▨ AD c.122–130 (broad wall)
▨ AD c.125–138 (narrow wall)
▨ AD c.125–138 gate blocking
▢ AD 170–270

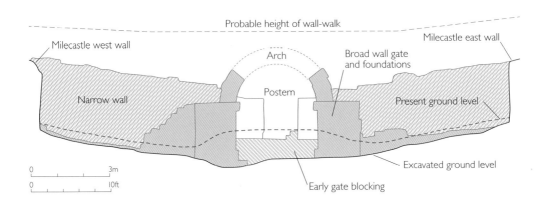

Probable height of wall-walk

Milecastle west wall

Milecastle east wall

Arch

Broad wall gate and foundations

Narrow wall

Postem

Present ground level

Excavated ground level

Early gate blocking

0   3m
0   10ft

Wall face undisturbed by later restoration and conservation. In the wall face there are two levelling courses of thin slabs. If a third were added at the same interval in height, this would suggest that the wall-walk of the milecastle was 4.5m high. This corresponds with the projected curve of the archway above the gate, and together they provide one of the key pieces of evidence for the height of the wall-walk of Hadrian's Wall. There is likely also to have been a parapet on the north side, which would have added to the overall height.

Soon after the gate was completed the foundations proved to be inadequate and the north arch slumped, blocking up the gateway. This was later reopened as a narrow postern. The milecastle remained occupied into the later fourth century. Among the stones used in the later flagged floor was a fragment of a building inscription originally set up by the second Augustan legion, stationed at Caerleon. This legion is known to have also built milecastles 38 and 42.

Milecastle 37

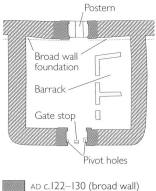

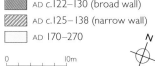

Postern
Broad wall foundation
Barrack
Gate stop
Pivot holes

AD c.122–130 (broad wall)
AD c.125–138 (narrow wall)
AD 170–270

0   10m
0   30ft

N

Above: *Reconstruction drawing of the milecastle as it would have appeared in the second century. The tower over the gate collapsed soon after it was built and was not replaced*
Left: *The interior of the milecastle seen from the south-west, showing the remains of the third-century barracks and the well-preserved north curtain wall and gate*

History of Housesteads

INVASION AND CONQUEST

Emperor Claudius invaded Britain in AD 43 and, despite some fierce resistance from the British tribes, the legions were able to control much of the island as far as southern Scotland by AD 80. By AD 84, after a major victory over the northern tribes, the empire reached its high tide of expansion beyond the river Tay and the edge of the Highlands. But within a few years control was relinquished as forces were required on the continental frontiers. Over the next 30 years garrisons were established between the Tweed and the Tyne, and from about AD 105 there appears to have been a greater emphasis on garrisons on the Tyne–Solway isthmus, between Corbridge, Vindolanda and Carlisle, although this was not yet a fortified frontier. Emperor Trajan (AD 98–117) conducted major wars of Roman aggression, with conquests in Dacia (Romania), in what is now Armenia and in Parthia (Iraq). His successor, Hadrian (AD 117–38), faced insurrections across the empire and abandoned further conquests in the east. There is evidence for warfare and increased military pressure in northern Britain and, following the emperor's visit to Britain in AD 122 construction work began on Hadrian's Wall.

Above: A bust of the emperor Claudius torn from a bronze statue and cast into the river Alde in Suffolk, probably after the sack of Colchester during the revolt of Boudicca in AD 60 or 61

Right: The tombstone of Flavinus from Hexham Abbey, showing a cavalry standard-bearer from the Ala Petriana regiment trampling a barbarian. This regiment was probably stationed at Corbridge in the late first century AD before Hadrian's Wall was built

Facing page: The bold sweep of Hadrian's Wall as it climbs onto Housesteads Crags. Although many of the wall stones have been reset the fabric of the wall remains Roman

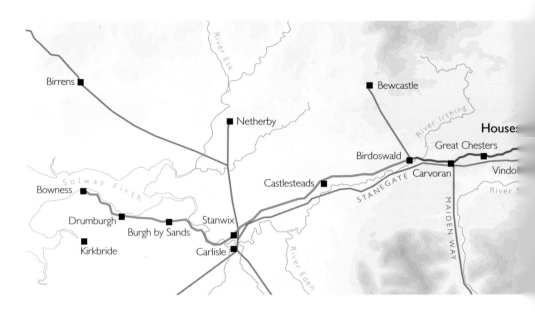

BUILDING HADRIAN'S WALL

The Wall was a new type of frontier unprecedented in the Roman world, a stone and turf wall constructed across the narrowest part of northern England. West of the river Irthing in Cumbria, the Wall was first built of turf, where good building stone was less widely available, and only later completed in stone. In the east and in the central sector of the Whin Sill Crags stone was used from the outset.

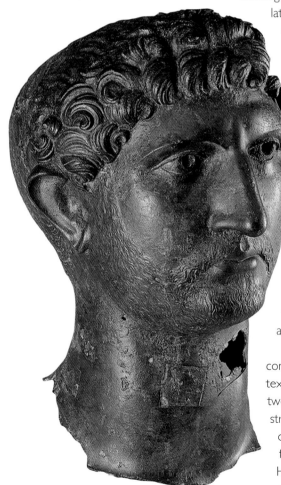

Initially the stone wall was built to a width of 10 Roman feet (3m), but at Housesteads only lengths of a broader foundation are known. After the laying out of the foundation came the construction of milecastles, regularly spaced approximately one Roman mile (1472m) apart. Between each of these were two towers, or turrets. The foundations of one (Turret 36B) are known at Housesteads. Owing to the extent of archaeological investigation over the past century to the east and west of Housesteads, more is known here about the way the Wall was constructed than anywhere else along its length (see page 6). There are few written sources about the construction of Hadrian's Wall; indeed the main text, the *Historia Augusta*, dates from at least two centuries later, but a careful analysis of the structural history allows a fuller understanding of how the Wall was built, and how it functioned. The garrison for the new fort at Housesteads may have been drawn from the

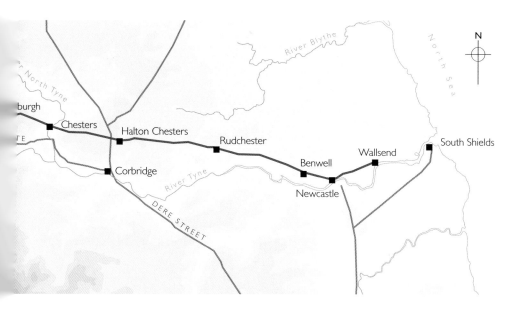

earlier fort of Vindolanda situated on the Stanegate to the south, but there is no direct evidence. Once the fort and Wall were complete, the great ditch and double banks of the Vallum were dug along the south side. Access across the Vallum was limited to the forts: at Housesteads a controlled crossing place is known but the line is masked by later terraces.

By the end of Hadrian's reign the system of the great Wall was complete. With nearly 15 forts and more than 10,000 men garrisoned along it, the Wall stood as a dramatic gesture of Roman military power intended to intimidate and divide the unconquered peoples of Britain and to ensure the security of the lands to the south.

Key to map of Hadrian's Wall

——— Hadrian's Wall
——— Hadrian's Wall
first built of turf
------- Roman road
■ Roman fort

Top: Map of Hadrian's Wall showing the forts and roads along the Wall
Left: Scene of legionaries building from Trajan's Column in Rome. Although the legionaries could be expected to carry out major building projects it is unlikely they worked in full armour as the column shows

Facing page: Head of the emperor Hadrian recovered from the Thames at London Bridge in 1834. The original statue probably stood in the forum in Roman London

Right: Latin inscription recording a
dedication to the gods and goddesses
by the First Cohort of Tungrians in
accordance with the interpretation of
the oracle of Apollo at Claros, in
modern Turkey

Below: Rim of a cooking vessel with
the name Neuto – a name only
found otherwise in Tungria –
scratched into it

Bottom: altar dedicated to the god
Silvanus Cocidius by the prefect of the
Tungrians, Quintus Florius Maternus

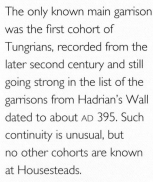

Names and Places

The only known main garrison
was the first cohort of
Tungrians, recorded from the
later second century and still
going strong in the list of the
garrisons from Hadrian's Wall
dated to about AD 395. Such
continuity is unusual, but
no other cohorts are known
at Housesteads.

Early in the third century
the garrison was strengthened
by a war band of Frisians
recruited from outside the
empire. One inscription
records a Cuneus Frisiorum
('wedge of Frisians') but on
another they are simply
identified by the name of their
leader as the *Numerus
Hnaudifridi*. They both
dedicated altars to the god
Mars Thincsus, and one
identifies the origin of the war
band as Twente in east
Holland. They brought with
them a particular form of

pottery, termed Housesteads
Ware, which was made locally
but used Frisian designs, an
example of which may be seen
in the museum.

Many personal names
survive on inscriptions or as
graffiti on stones or pots. Some
are standard Romanized British
names, but other names with
three parts refer to the officers
who belonged to the equestrian
order, such as Quintus Florius
Maternus from Colchester. Of
particular interest are the
German names connected to
the Tungrians. It is often thought
that over time the Roman army
increasingly recruited locally.
However, one name, Neuto,
scratched into the side of a
third-century pot-sherd, has
parallels only from Tungria itself
and implies that the regiment
retained strong connections to
its homeland long after its
creation in the first century AD.

Left: View of Watling Lodge, a Roman fort on the Antonine Wall built along the Forth–Clyde isthmus from AD 142 but abandoned by AD 158
Below: View of the south-west angle of the fort showing repairs using long stone blocks. Similar work elsewhere on the walls indicates continuing concern for the fort's security

AFTER HADRIAN TO THE THIRD CENTURY

Almost as soon as Hadrian's Wall was complete, Hadrian's successor Antoninus Pius (r. AD 138–161) advanced Roman frontiers once more into Scotland. Construction began in AD 142 of a new barrier built of turf and timber, the Antonine Wall, across the Forth–Clyde isthmus in central Scotland. It is often thought that Hadrian's Wall was then abandoned, but recent excavations at Housesteads did not find any evidence of this, so it seems that part of the garrison may have remained here. In any event the Scottish venture was short-lived and before the death of its builder, by AD 158, the Antonine Wall was abandoned and Hadrian's Wall was once more occupied in force, with only outpost forts to the north.

Some buildings at Housesteads show evidence of modifications and repairs, including the hospital, and the latrines, which acquired a major new cistern. An inscription

Above: *Reconstruction of a large building inscription from about AD 205–08, probably relating to the newly constructed double granary. The fragmentary pieces were found in later rebuilding. 'For the Emperor-Caesars Lucius Septimius Severus Pius Pertinax, Augustus, and Marcus Aurelius Antoninus Pius, Augustus, and for Publius Septimius Geta, most noble Caesar, the First Cohort of Tungrians, 1,000 strong, restored [this building] by order of Lucius Alfenius Senecio, imperial propraetorian legate.'*

Below: *Fragmentary inscription recording 'the decree of the vicani' (villagers), showing that the civilian community had some sort of formal status. The settlement appears to have flourished for more than a century but appears to have been abandoned after AD 270*

from the time of Septimius Severus (r. AD 193–211) found in fragments in various later rebuilds probably relates to the reconstruction of the granaries as two separate buildings. The layout of most of the barracks remained unchanged, but the rampart banks were removed in many places to provide space for metal workshops, although to compensate elsewhere some stretches of the curtain wall were widened. Early in the third century the Vallum was no longer maintained as a barrier and the civilian settlement probably expanded, as the new house fronts were built across part of the main roadway leading from the south gate. The Knag Burn gate replaced the north gate as the main access through Hadrian's Wall.

Only a few of these changes can be dated with certainty, but throughout this period of more than a century it appears that neither the main garrison nor the *vicus* reduced in size. Despite its remote location the garrison of Tungrians, now augmented by the Frisian war bands, and civilian population could survive and even flourish, owing to the resources of the command economy of the Roman State.

THE LATER EMPIRE

During the later third and fourth centuries imperial defence was no longer so reliant on the legions and auxiliaries in the frontier provinces such as north Britain, and the emperors came to depend on field armies stationed throughout the empire. It is likely that the overall strength of the garrison diminished and some of the soldiers' dependants moved inside the fort, but no direct evidence has been found.

After AD 270 the civilian settlement outside the fort walls appears to have been abandoned, although is not clear where the inhabitants moved to. The few later coins found at buildings close to the south gate were probably lost by accident in this area, and are not indications that the buildings were occupied at this time. The change may reflect the more direct involvement of the State in the provisioning of the garrison, as indicated by the new building 15. The main concern was to provide new accommodation for the soldiers, and strengthen the fort's defences. The walls and ramparts

Roman Religion

The Romans worshipped many gods: some were the deities of the State, the cult of the emperor and the major Olympian gods, especially Iupiter Optimus Maximus – 'Jupiter the best and greatest'. Also popular were gods such as Mars, god of War, and the patron of soldiers; Mercury, the messenger god, protector of traders, who is known from the *vicus*, and the marine god Neptune, seen in statues found near the latrines. Others reflected local cults and spirits belonging to native traditions; discovered in a *vicus* shrine the *genii cucullati* – a triad of hooded figures wrapped up against the north winds – were established gods found across

Britain and the western provinces of the empire. Other dedications, for example to the Veteres, have no antecedents and emerged as a new cult.

Sculptures and inscriptions provide evidence of religion and worship. One inscription is a dedication to the gods and goddesses in accordance with the interpretation of the oracle at Claros, today in western Turkey. Ten similar dedications survive across the empire from southern Turkey, Mauretania in north Africa and Sardinia and have been associated with the outbreak of plague around 165, in the reign of Marcus Aurelius.

The Frisians built a temple on the north flank of Chapel Hill to their god Mars Thincsus and his female attendants the Alaisiagae, who later appear as the Valkyries of German mythology. Temples to Mithras

were built partly underground and were set apart to enhance their exclusivity and mystery. Mithras was an eastern deity whose cult was popular in the Roman army. Most impressive from all the surviving sculptures is the relief representing the birth of the god Mithras, shown emerging from the egg of creation and framed by the cosmos.

Above: Stone relief showing the birth of Mithras from an egg – the symbol of Eternal Time. The god is framed by an egg-shaped zodiac representing the cosmos and would have been lit from behind

Left: Inscribed pillar from a temple at Chapel Hill dedicated to the German war god, Mars Thincsus, his attendants and to the Deity of the Emperor by Germans originating from Frisia (north-east Holland)

were repaired and new interval towers built, giving the fort a more dramatic, multi-turreted appearance. New earthworks dug across the west side completely blocked the west gate. Inside the fort, all the barracks were transformed into rows of individual dwellings ('chalets'). Later in the fourth century the defences were further modified as timber towers replaced stone platforms and the earth rampart encroached across the perimeter road. The small baths at the end of building 15 probably replaced the earlier baths situated outside the fort, perhaps reflecting greater concern for security.

Military occupation continued up to the end of the fourth century, although there are just a few traces of immediate post-Roman structures among a pattern of dereliction. One very late feature was an apsidal building, probably a church and similar in plan to a building recently excavated at Vindolanda. It may relate to the 'cist' burial inside an earlier stone cistern, close to the north rampart. Once imperial authority ended and external resources ceased to reach Housesteads, the garrison and its community were forced to leave a place capable of sustaining only a sparse population.

Above: The water tank close to the north rampart. Inside are stone settings for a 'cist' burial. This dates from the immediate post-Roman period and can be associated with the remains of a church, located to the east but no longer visible
Right: A medieval view of Hadrian's Wall, as seen in this 13th-century map prepared by Matthew Paris

Facing page: Housesteads under snow, seen from the east. The modern field wall in the foreground follows the course of the Wall. Traces of the military way cross the fields towards the valley of the Knag Burn, marked by trees, and on to the fort

Right: John Armstrong's Last Goodnight, *from a 17th-century ballad about one of the notorious Scots Armstrongs who were harried out of Liddesdale by James VI. Some settled in Northumberland and were infamous troublemakers*

Below: Map showing the border country between England and Scotland in the 16th century. Administrative areas known in both countries as the 'marches' evolved in the Middle Ages

A TUDOR FRONTIER

The name 'House steads' is first recorded in the 16th century and the Knag Burn appears in a list of 'Border watches' in 1542, as one of the lookouts set up along the Anglo–Scottish borderlands. Throughout the Middle Ages the fort and much of the Wall along the crags westwards lay on the southern edge of the great 'waste' which extended as far as the modern Scottish border. Used for hunting and seasonal pasture, by the 16th century these lands lay in the Middle March between England and Scotland, and Housesteads became notorious for the thieves known as 'moss troopers' who thrived in the region. This reputation continued even after the Union of the Crowns in 1603; in the following year Hugh Nixon from Housesteads is

Key

✚ Abbey
🏰 Castle
⚔ Site of battle

0 _____ 25km
0 _____ 15mi

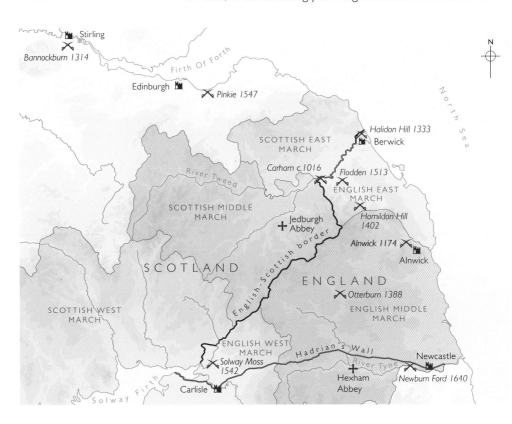

Left: The ruins of Black Middens bastle house, a type of defensible farmhouse, in the Tarset Valley, Northumberland. Buildings such as this are found on both sides of the Anglo–Scottish border

Below: The earliest illustration of Housesteads by William Stukeley in 1725. Stukeley described the many sculptures and inscriptions on Chapel Hill (in the foreground) as 'a cumulus of Roman antiquities'

recorded as 'a stealer of cattle and receiver of stolen goods'. Later in the century the lands were tenanted by the Armstrongs who were described as 'a great nuisance in the county, frightening people in their houses and taking what they liked'. By 1698 the rule of law had closed in sufficiently to force the sale of Housesteads to Thomas Gibson of Hexham, and for some of the Armstrong family to seek their fortunes in America.

The late medieval settlement was centred in the south-east part of the fort. Traces of a long house survive across the interior of the south gate and the stone of the east gate tower was reused to build part of a bastle house, a two-storey defensible farmhouse. These dwellings are characteristic of the Border regions and provided secure shelter for livestock in a ground-floor byre with accommodation for the family above. Farms were later located inside the fort, one on the site of the hospital and shown in a sketch by William Stukeley, and a contemporary corn-drying kiln can be seen in the south granary.

A Cumulus of Roman Antiquitys at Housteads.

William Camden

'I could not safely take a full survey of it for fear of the rank robbers thereabouts'

Above: Detail from a portrait of William Camden, an antiquarian who visited the Wall in 1599, by or after Marcus Gheeraerts the Younger, 1609

Below: View of the aedes, *or shrine, within the headquarters building, looking north. The photograph was taken in 1898 during excavations and the columns were collected from across the fort*

ANTIQUARIANS AND ARCHAEOLOGISTS

The notorious reputation of the district deterred all but the boldest of Elizabethan antiquarians. William Camden, who visited the Roman Wall in 1599, dared not go to Housesteads and nearby Busy Gap writing that 'I could not safely take a full survey of it for fear of the rank robbers thereabouts'. But within four years of Gibson buying Housesteads, the wealth and variety of the Roman antiquities was recognized and it soon became established as 'the most remarkable and magnificent station in the whole island'. The earliest excavations for inscriptions and sculptures, by Alexander Gordon and John Clerk of Penicuik, date from 1724 and in the following year Stukeley wrote that the remains were 'as ruined but yesterday'. His sketch evokes a landscape littered with ancient statuary and inscriptions which so appealed to the classically educated 18th-century visitor. The first systematic description was published by John Horsley in his *Britannia Romana* (1732).

The first scientific excavations were undertaken by the Northumbrian antiquarian and historian John Hodgson. Following the discovery of the Mithraeum in 1822, he investigated the south, east and west gates, as well as the small bathhouse in building 15. In 1838 the farm and its land were sold to John Clayton of Chesters to become the jewel in his Roman Wall estate. At the time of his death in 1892, aged 98, this comprised five forts and many miles of Wall along the crags, one of the earliest examples in Britain of an individual acquiring land in order to ensure the preservation and display of archaeological remains. Throughout the middle decades of the mid 19th century his workmen cleared the walls of the fort and those lengths of Hadrian's Wall now capped with turf. Although little was recorded from these 'diggings', his legacy was to ensure the survival of the Wall on his estate and to maintain Housesteads' international reputation as the principal fort on the Wall for tourists and scholars alike.

Collections

Since the 18th century the fort and surrounding fields have provided a rich harvest of carved stones and inscriptions, together with pottery and artefacts from excavations. The Gibsons formed the first collection at their house at Stagshaw, which became the nucleus of the Newcastle Society of Antiquaries' collection, now housed in the Great North Museum. John Clayton also formed his own collection at his house at Chesters and shortly after his death in 1892 a purpose-built museum was built close to Chesters Roman Fort.

At Housesteads the site museum was created in 1936 by the National Trust to house the finds from the excavations of the *vicus*. The new building was deliberately planned as a reconstruction of one of the recently excavated buildings from the *vicus* – building 8, the 'Murder House'.

Finds from Housesteads

1. Two jet beads from the commanding officer's house
2. Amber bead
3. Lithomarge spindlewhorl
4. Copper alloy finger ring
5. Jet or shale ring
6. Silver finger ring
7. Bone hook
8. Disc brooch from north-east corner of the fort
9. Enamelled disc brooch from north curtain wall
10. Disc brooch from north curtain wall
11. Enamelled disc brooch
12. Copper-alloy wheel brooch
13. Jet hair ornament (possible)
14. Silver earring
15. Silver pin
16. Part of jet or shale pin
17. Part of a harness (possible)
18. Samian bowl stamped 'Ianus'
19. Fragment of window glass
20. Enamelled flask

Right: Building the Roman Wall
from the 'History of Northumbria'
paintings by William Bell Scott, now
in the central hall at Wallington,
near Morpeth. The Roman officer was
modelled on John Clayton, who
bought the Housesteads estate and
ensured the Wall's survival in the
19th century
Below: The archaeologist
RC Bosanquet (standing centre back)
and his workers at the south gate at
Housesteads in 1898

Excavations in 1898 sponsored by the Newcastle Society of
Antiquaries systematically explored the internal buildings of the
fort and provided one of the first plans of a fort from
anywhere in the Roman empire. The works were directed by a
young academic, RC Bosanquet, and marked a transition from
the era of gentlemen antiquaries to professional archaeologists.
After the sale of the Clayton Estate in Northumberland in
1931, Housesteads Fort was given to the National Trust,
although the farm and its land were not acquired until 1974.
Professor Eric Birley excavated milecastle 37 and the civilian
settlement, one of the earliest excavations of a *vicus* in any of
the Hadrian's Wall forts.